WALKING CLOS

the DUKERIES
(Sherwood Forest)

Number Forty Two in the popular series of walking guides

Contents

Walk		Miles	Page No
1	Lindrick Dale	6	4
2	New Plantation	7½	6
3	Spitfire Hill	5¾	8
4	Clumber Park	6¼	10
5	Boughton Brake	6¾	12
6	Creswell Crags	9¼	14
7	Chequer Bridge	4¾	16
8	Swinston Hill Wood	7¼	18
9	Hanger Hill Drive	7½	20
10	Pleasley Vale	5¼	22
11	Rhodesia	5½	24
12	The Meden and the Maun	7	26

Walked, Written and Drawn by Clive Brown
© Clive Brown 2007 – 2013

Published by Clive Brown
ISBN 978-1-907669-42-2

PLEASE
Take care of the countryside
Your leisure is someone's livelihood

Close gates
Start no fires
Keep away from livestock and animals
Do not stray from marked paths
Take litter home
Do not damage walls, hedgerows or fences
Cross only at stiles or gates
Protect plants, trees and wildlife
Keep dogs on leads
Respect crops, machinery and rural property
Do not contaminate water

Although not essential we recommend good walking boots; during hot weather take something to drink on the way. All walks can easily be negotiated by an averagely fit person. The routes have been recently walked and surveyed, changes can however occur, please follow any signed diversions. Some paths cross fields which are under cultivation. All distances and times are approximate.

The maps give an accurate portrayal of the area, but scale has however been sacrificed in some cases for the sake of clarity and to fit restrictions of page size.

Walking Close To have taken every care in the research and production of this guide but cannot be held responsible for the safety of anyone using them.

During very wet weather, parts of these walks may become impassable through flooding, check before starting out. Stiles and rights of way can get overgrown during the summer; folding secateurs are a useful addition to a walker's rucksack.

Thanks to Angela for help in production of these booklets

Views or comments?
walkingcloseto@yahoo.co.uk

Reproduced from Ordnance Survey Mapping on behalf of The Controller of Her Majesty's Stationery Office. © Crown Copyright License No. 100037980.

Walking Close to the Dukeries

The Dukeries takes its name from the cluster of stately homes south of Worksop. Clumber Park, the ancestral seat of the Dukes of Newcastle; Welbeck Abbey, home of the Dukes of Portland and Thoresby Hall, once the seat of the Dukes of Kingston. It was unusual in having the properties of more than one duke in a county and even more unusual in having the properties so close together, the borders often joining. The Clumber Park mansion was demolished after a fire in 1938, Welbeck Abbey is now the Army sixth ford college and Thoresby Hall has become a hotel.

Worksop Manor came into the family of the Dukes of Norfolk through marriage but was little used. In 1840 the 12th Duke sold it to the Duke of Newcastle, who bought it just to increase the size of the Clumber Park estate. The house was partly demolished and rebuilt towards the end of the century. The Dukes of Leeds also owned a house locally at Kiveton; this was demolished in 1812, reputedly as a result of a bet with the Prince of Wales.

The eccentric William Cavendish-Scott-Bentinck (1800-1879) became the fifth Duke of Portland on the death of his father in 1854. He hated meeting people so created a network of tunnels and underground rooms in Welbeck Park (walk no 6), the largest of which, oddly enough was a massive ballroom. He communicated with most people by letter and the servants had strict instructions not to look at him or acknowledge his presence if they met him by accident. If he had business in London his coach, with the windows blanked out, would be driven to Worksop station, where it was loaded on a truck so the Duke could travel in total seclusion. The tunnels were lit by gas and had thick skylights; they are marked on OS maps but are difficult to see on the ground. The Dukedom became extinct in 1990.

The caves in Creswell Crags (walk no 6) were used as shelter during the Ice Age ten thousand years ago, some of the artwork painted then can be seen in the Church Hole and Robin Hood caves. Evidence of Ice Age man has also been found in Lindrick Dale (walk no 1).

The River Meden and the River Maun (walk no 12) both flow east to west across Nottinghamshire before merging temporarily near Bothamsall. They divide after a short distance and go on separately to a point near Markham Moor where they once more combine to form the River Idle.

We feel that it would be difficult to get lost with the instructions and maps in this booklet, but please take care it is obviously much easier to get lost in trees than in open countryside. We recommend carrying an Ordnance Survey map, the walks are on Explorer Map Nos 270 and 279; Landranger No. 120 covers at a smaller scale. Roads, geographical features and buildings, not on our map but visible from the walk can be easily identified.

1   Lindrick Dale

    6 Miles   3 Hours

Use the parking area on the outskirts of South Anston (B6059) Crowgate. Free but no facilities, shops in the village.

1 Turn right out of the entrance, back towards the village, past the bus stop and turn right into Windsor Walk. At Lordswood Avenue turn right, then left into High Ash Drive and right into Azalea Close. At the end turn left at the signpost and follow the left hand field edge with the houses to the left up to the T-junction of paths.

2 Take the field edge to the right and continue down the left hand side of the long narrow sloping field. Keep direction on the track between fields, down through the trees, cross carefully over the railway and turn left along the towpath of the Chesterfield Canal.

3 Walk along the towpath for a mile and a quarter, past Thorpe Treble Lock; go under Bridge 35, turn around, climb over the ladder stile and take the track to the right downhill away from the canal.

4 Cross over the railway and bear right across the open field, which may be under cultivation although a path should be visible within any crop. Take the hardcore farm road left at the signpost over the bridge across the disused railway and past the houses. Turn right through the bridge under the railway up the wide hardcore road and bear left to the signpost; turn right, then bear immediate left uphill.

5 Go past the golf club sign and turn sharp left through the high undergrowth, Continue ahead along the edge of the golf course, with the hedge to the left and the driveway, up to the A57. Cross this busy road with care and turn left along the roadside path to the signpost on the uphill slope. Turn right, carry on along the more established path ahead and bear left down the slope.

6 At the Anston Stones Wood sign bear right over the footbridge, turn right and go up the shallow steps of the left hand track. Bear left up the sleeper steps and continue on the path through the grassy area with the trees to the left. Go up a set of steps on the right, go through a gap and carry on ahead with the trees to the left. Continue with a green fence now right and keep on this path more or less straight on, to the road close to the railway bridge.

7 Turn left under the railway and turn immediate right along a path parallel to the railway, turn left at the end along the path to the road. Cross and continue on the path straight on to the road by the Methodist church. Keep left/straight on along the road ahead all the way to the car park on the left and your vehicle.

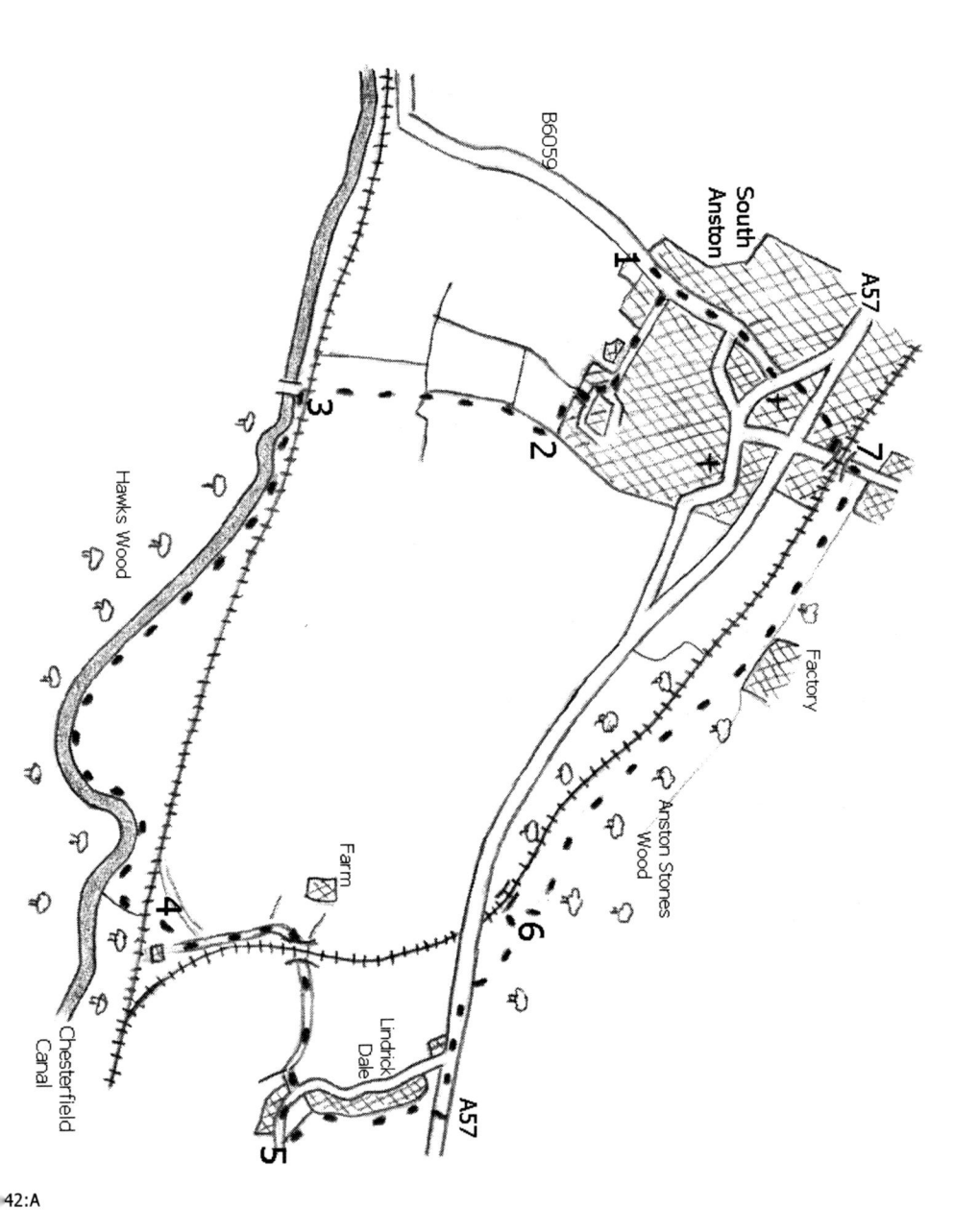

The unique barges used on the Chesterfield Canal, always horse drawn during their working life and never brightly painted, were nicknamed 'cuckoos'; the walk along the canal path has been promoted as the 'Cuckoo Way'.

2 New Plantation

$7^1/_2$ Miles $3^1/_4$ Hours

Use one of the car parks in the centre of Market Warsop, toilets and all other facilities adjacent.

1 Go out of town along Mansfield Road for just over a quarter of a mile, turn right into Vale Avenue and fork left into Sookholme Lane. Continue direction along the hardcore bridleway over the River Meden at Hammerwater Bridge and underneath the railway.

2 Just past Herrings Farm turn right, carry on ahead down the tree lined path and follow the grass track between fields to the road. Turn right under William Wood Bridge and immediate left past the pub along the rough road with the houses to the right. Go through the bollards and carry on to the metal gate just past William Wood Farm.

3 Turn left through the narrow gate along the track on the right hand field edge with the hedge to the right. Cross the stile, go into the next corner and turn right up the wide track, keep ahead over a stile to the signpost close to the corner and take the path left through the trees.

4 Exit the trees, turn right along the field edge to the boundary and follow the field edge to the left with the hedge to the right. At the corner cross the open field ahead which may be under cultivation although a track should be well marked (it may be easier around the edge of the field), to the yellow top post.

5 Go down the steps into the disused railway cutting and left up the steps on the other side. Keep ahead through the trees and maintain direction on the rutted track through New Plantation to the railway bridge. Turn sharp right on the wide stony path with the trees to the right to a crossroads of paths.

6 Turn right along the overgrown path between the trees and the wall past Top Farm and continue over a stile up the narrow path between hedges. Follow the path right and then left up a slope. Keep direction between the wire fence and the hedge into Cuckney Hay Wood to the crossroads of paths.

7 Turn right and fork left at the junction; at the next fork go left and carry on to the road. Turn right and walk between the old bridge piers to the signpost close to the red barrier. Take the path not signposted, veering away from then running parallel to the road. Join the road right/ahead for 150yds; turn right at the signpost and walk down to the B6031.

Completed on the next Page (Eight)

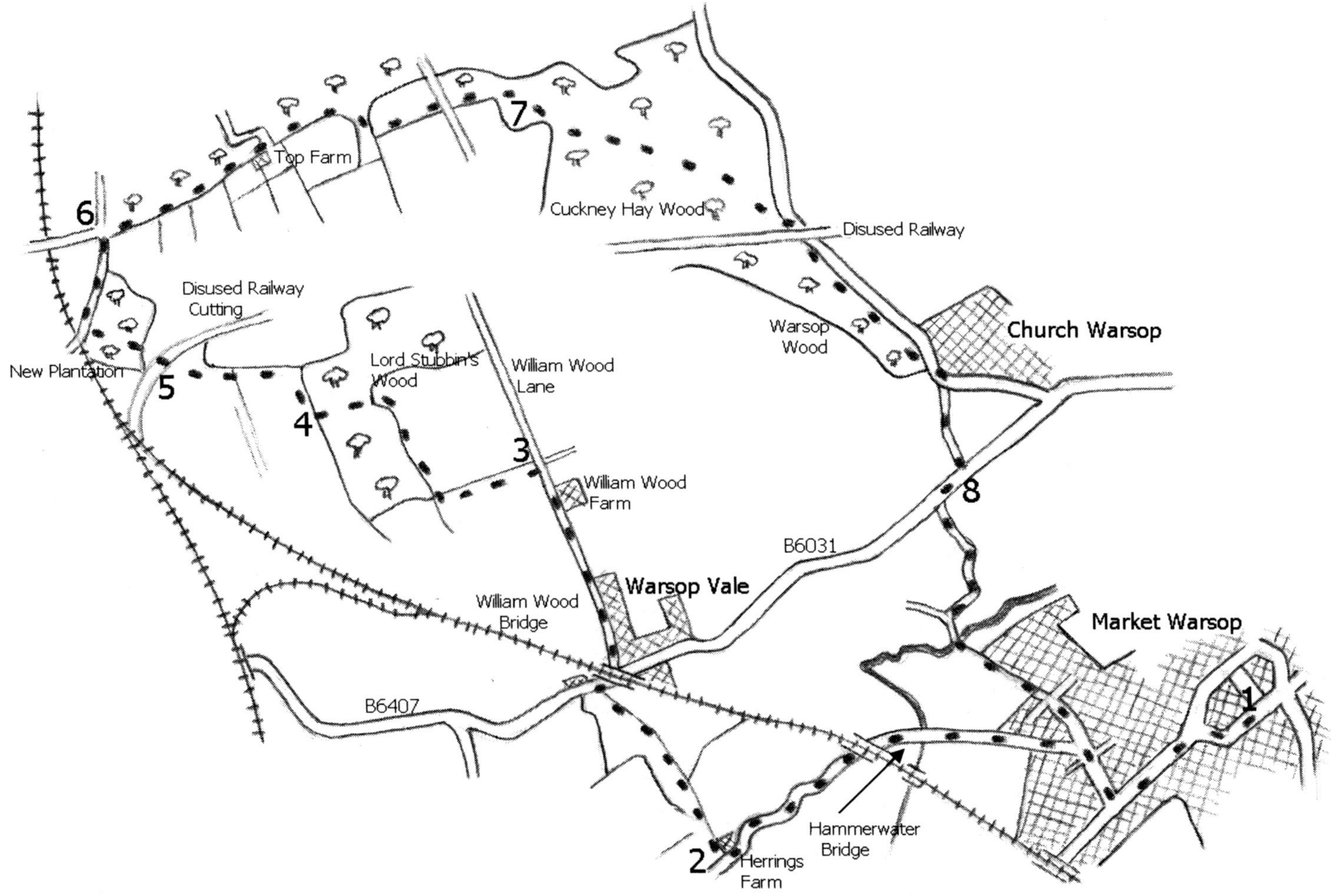

6
Top Farm
7
Cuckney Hay Wood
Disused Railway
Disused Railway
Cutting
New Plantation
5
4
Lord Stubbin's
Wood
William Wood
Lane
3
William Wood
Farm
Warsop
Wood
Church Warsop
8
B6031
Warsop Vale
William Wood
Bridge
Market Warsop
1
B6407
Hammerwater
Bridge
2
Herrings
Farm

Completion of 2 New Plantation from the previous Page

8   Take the road right for 90yds to the signpost and turn left down the hedged bridleway to the road. Turn right for 75yds and left at the signpost; go straight on at the signpost through the bushes, over the footbridge and keep direction with the houses to the left. Bear right with Stonebridge Lane and walk up to Mansfield Road. Turn back into Market Warsop town centre to find your vehicle.

3   Spitfire Hill

$5^3/_4$ Miles $2^1/_4$ Hours

Use the car park in Hardwick village in Clumber Park, toilets, but all other facilities at the main site. The park is free but there is an entry charge for vehicles.

1   Walk back to the T-junction at the entrance and turn left up the slope to the marker post just short of the houses. Turn right, follow the farm track through the trees and bear right with the trees to the right. Continue through the gate into the trees, at marker post 11 go straight on to the A614 and cross this busy road carefully.

2   Maintain direction between hedges and carry on along the wide field edge with the hedge to the left. Keep ahead on this track under the wires and through the trees. Continue parallel with the telegraph poles past Crookford Farm to the road.

3   Turn right and keep straight on over the footbridge next to the ford, carry on along the track and bear right between the two posts marked by arrow discs. Turn left along the wide path between trees parallel with the telegraph poles, the land rises gently to the right, to the low, wooded summit of Spitfire Hill. Continue over the field still next to the telegraph poles to the road and turn right.

4   Keep direction past the barrier through the trees all the way to the A614 and cross carefully into the Clumber Park entrance.

5   Turn right, before the gate at the low marker post, follow the permissive path left and right, cross the estate road and go through the narrow gateway. Bear left over the field which may be under cultivation although a path should be well marked, along the edge of the trees and down to the bottom corner. Take the road right, over the footbridge next to the ford to the junction at Hardwick. Turn left back to the car park and your vehicle.

Hardwick

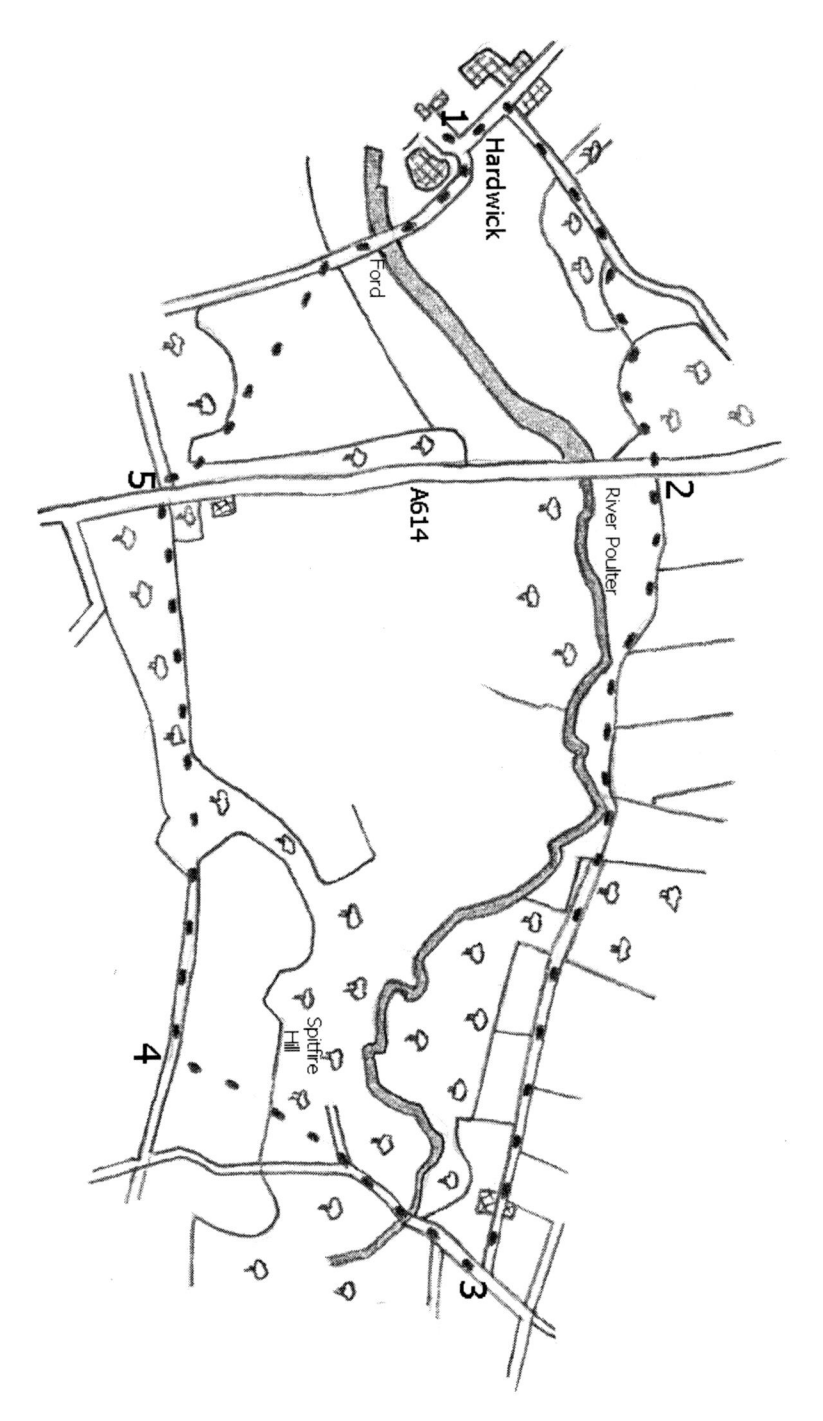

Ford

A614

River Poulter

Spitfire Hill

42:A

Page Nine

4 Clumber Park

6 Miles $2^1/_2$ Hours

Use the car park in Hardwick village in Clumber Park, toilets, but all other facilities at the main site. The park is free but there is an entry charge for vehicles.

1 Go back to the road and turn left uphill along the entrance road. After half a mile bear left at the bridleway sign along the path through the trees. Keep direction over the estate road to the more substantial path at the marker post and bear right, with the open ground to the left.

2 Continue straight on through the lines of trees at Limetree Avenue and maintain direction across the next road through the trees to the red brick cottages on the right.

3 Turn sharp left on the hardcore road, still between the trees; cross the road ahead and carry on to the cycleway signpost. Turn right, follow this track and take the estate road to the left. Bear right at the wooden barrier and follow this tarmac estate road over the cattle grid and past the next barrier to Limetree Avenue.

4 Keep direction across this staggered junction and go straight on at the fork. Continue along the road bearing slight left and cross over Clumber Bridge.

5 Turn left on the path around the edge of the lake all the way to the buildings at Hardwick village and your vehicle in the car park.

The magnificent mansion at Clumber Park was demolished after a disastrous fire in 1938, when the Duke of Newcastle could not afford to rebuild it. The 3800 acre park has been in the care of the National Trust since 1946. Two impressive buildings remain, the two storey stable block which is used as offices by the National Trust and a Gothic Revival Chapel with an 180ft high spire, built for the 7th Duke in 1886 at a cost of £30,000. The park contains an 87 acre lake fed and drained by the River Poulter and a three mile long double limetree avenue, the longest in Europe. The Dukedom became extinct with the death of the 10th Duke in 1988.

Clumber Park is a paradise for birdwatchers as it consists of a wide range of habitats; there is the possibility of seeing up to 70 species in a single day, including some real rarities. Winter is a good time to visit as more reclusive birds can be seen in the leafless trees.

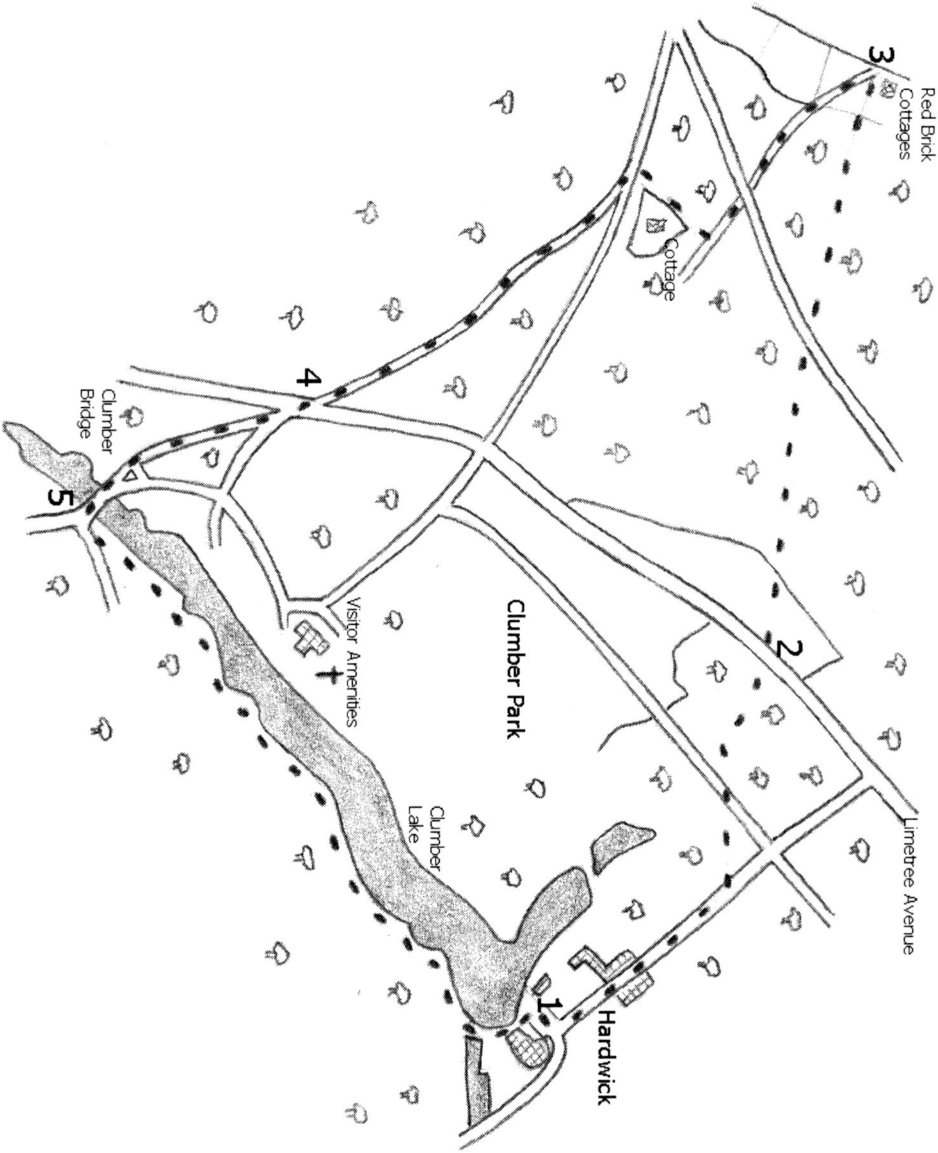
3
Red Brick
Cottages
Cottage
4
2
Clumber
Bridge
5
Visitor Amenities
Clumber Park
Clumber
Lake
Limetree Avenue
1
Hardwick

5   Boughton Brake

$6^3/_4$ Miles $3^1/_4$ Hours

Use the parking area north of Boughton Pumping Station (signposted from the A616 and A6075 in Ollerton and Boughton). Most facilities in the villages.

1   Take the main track north through Boughton Brake, bearing left; bear left at the fork and keep direction to the T-junction of roads at the corner of the wood. Turn left and immediate right through the narrow metal gate at the signpost and follow the path ahead with the fence to the right.

2   As the wooden fences end, turn right between the conifers and the wire fence. Bear right as this fence ends and turn right between the hedge and the trees, continue up to the corner and turn left. Follow the wide track between the farm buildings all the way to the road.

3   Turn left along the roadside path for 400yds and turn right through the wide hedge gap on the right. Take the path away from the road on the right hand field edge, with the hedge to the right. Continue over the farm road at the signpost and keep ahead to the footbridge.

4   Cross and turn right with the brook to the right up to the boundary. Go over the gate on the left rather than the water bound stile and exit over the stile at the far right. Turn left up to the T-junction and take the wide path to the right at the signpost. Keep direction on enclosed paths and field edges to a stile marked by a disc, next to a wide metal gate. Bear right, up the slope and step over the stile on to the road, turn right into Kirton village and go right/straight on at the junction.

5   Go past the 'Fox' to the footpath signpost on the right, step over the stile and walk down the right hand field edge. Cross the stile and turn right through the gateway along the right hand field edge. Continue through the gateway/bridge, bear left over the stile and go up the fenced track, step over the stile on the left and go up the right hand field edge to the gate on the right. Pass through and turn left, back to the original direction, through the wooden gate next to the wider metal gate.

6   Cross the road and continue ahead along the field edge with the hedge to the left to the next road at a corner. Follow the road left/straight on over the railway bridge to the corner of Boughton Brake. Take the track left through the edge of the trees leading back to the parking area and your vehicle.

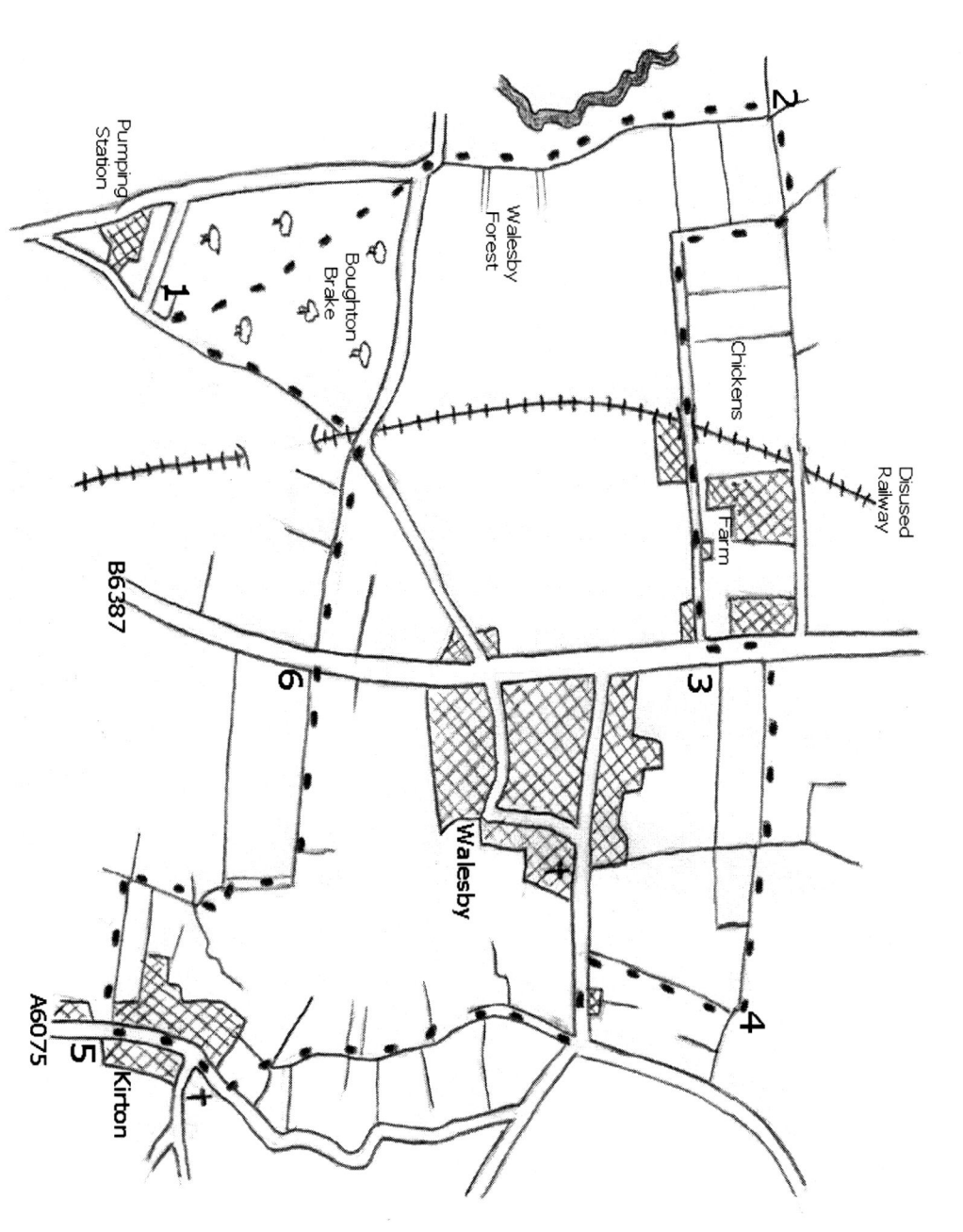

Boughton Pumping Station was built in 1907 to pump water into Nottingham, it was disused from the 1970s and after being left empty and derelict, it was reopened in 1998 as a business and conference centre.

Page Thirteen

6 Creswell Crags

9¼ Miles   4½ Hours

Use the car park at Creswell Crags, off the B6042 between the A60 and the A616 east of Creswell. Toilets and visitor centre, pay and display.

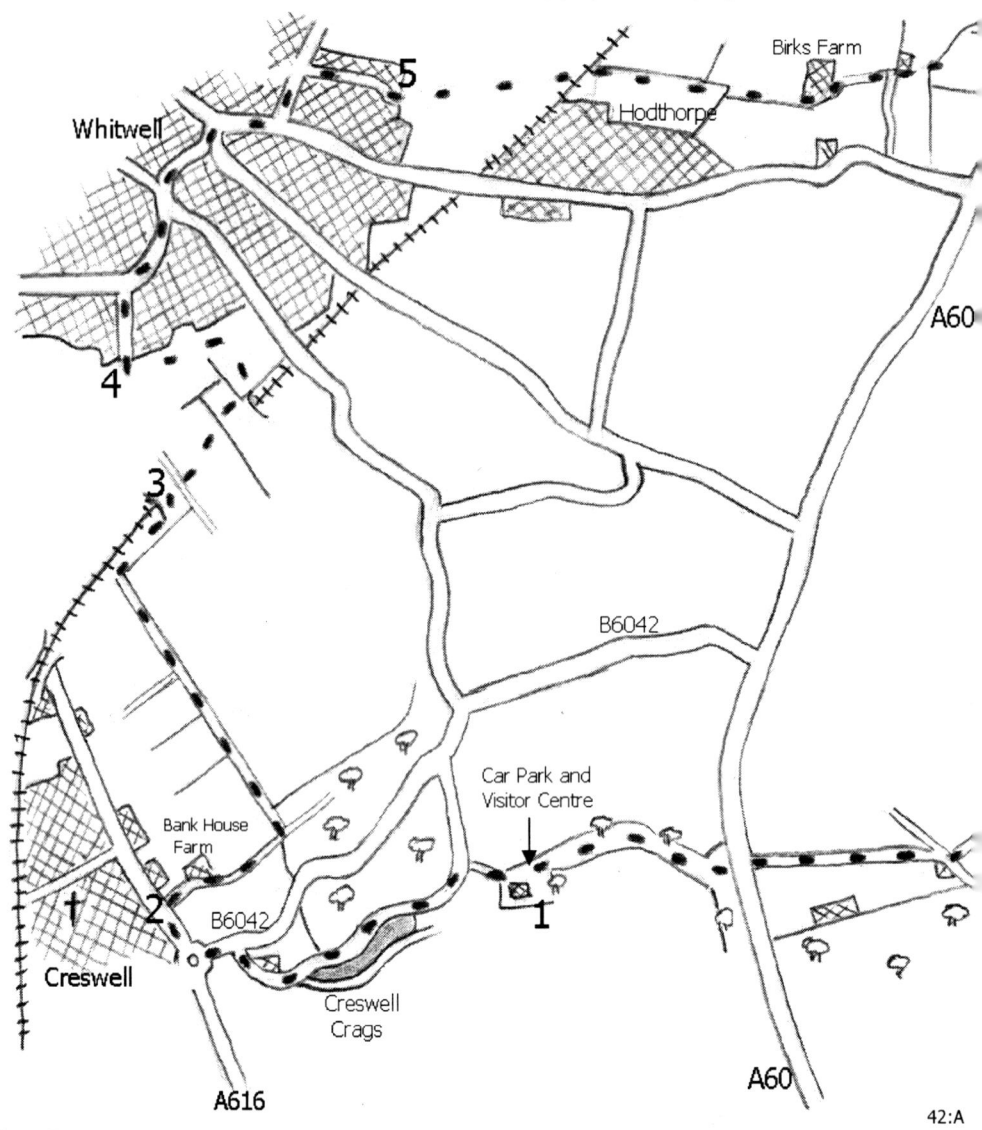

1 Walk past the visitor centre and take the path to the Crags, follow either of the paths through and continue towards Creswell. Bear left at the 30 signs and turn right at the roundabout for 150yds to the bridleway signpost.

2 Turn right and take the track right of Bank House Farm, parallel to the B6042. At the top of the rise, turn left at an unmarked point and double back a short way; turn right on the path through the trees between the wall and the fence. Cross the stile and keep direction on the right hand field edge, turn right parallel with the railway up the steps and the slope and turn left at the corner of the metal fence.

3 Turn almost immediate right over the quarry road and through the kissing gate, keep ahead, fork left at the junction in the grass and continue across the remains of a stone wall. Bear left through the kissing gate close to the further tunnel portal. Turn left up the slope on the track in the grass and follow the top of the ridge to the left. Turn right down the path into Whitwell.

4 Carry on ahead to the crossroads and turn right, follow this road into Titchfield Street and keep on this road as it becomes Hangar Hill. Go past the footpath signpost and turn left at the junction (still Hangar Hill), walk up to Mill Lane and turn right. At the end of the road, bear right past the footpath sign in the right hand corner and follow the footpath past the bungalow.

5 Continue ahead across the field which may be under cultivation although a path should be well marked within any crop. Cross back over the railway and the next narrow field, keep direction over the stiles to the right of the Birks Farm buildings to the tarmac farm road and turn left with the wooden fence to the right past a marker disc. Turn right at the gate and step over the stile, turn left past the stable, cross the next stile and continue up the slope on the wide track between fences between the houses and the bungalow. As this farm track swings left, cross over the stile next to the gate and maintain direction to the A60.

6 Cross this busy road carefully and continue along the track ahead over the footbridge in the hedge gap. Bear left on the path between fields and turn right
Completed on the next Page (Sixteen)

Page Fifteen

Completion of 6 Creswell Crags from the previous Page

with the hedge to the left up to the corner. Go through the gap and turn left through the gate, carry on along the farm track, pass through the next wide gate on the field edge with the trees to the left. Cross the footbridge and take the field edge to the left up to the stile, step over and turn right along the wide grass bridleway between hedges.

7 After a quarter of a mile at the crossroads turn right, follow this estate road to the left and carry on ahead to the trees. Go through the gate and follow the wide path through the trees, at the end keep right of South Lodge and turn left for 40yds along the hardcore road. Go past the ornate estate bungalow and turn right; bear right through a narrow gate for 50yds then turn left through the next narrow gate, past the Robin Hood Way marker disc.

8 Take the farm track ahead, between fields, bear right over the causeway between the lakes and turn right along the tarmac drive. Follow the drive left and right to the marker post and turn left upslope between hedges. Keep on this track to the concrete road at the signpost.

9 Turn right, follow the road left and go straight on at the crossroads. Carry on along the road to the A60, cross carefully and keep direction ahead past the house on the wide track through the trees leading eventually to the Creswell Crags car park and your vehicle.

7   Chequer Bridge

$4^3/_4$ Miles $2^1/_4$ Hours

Park at the north end of Ranby, on the old stretch of road next to the A1 and close to the village hall. No toilets, other facilities in the village.

1 Go very carefully over the A1 at the crossing point and follow the tarmac bridleway right/ahead over the cattle grid. Keep on this road (Thievesdale Lane), over Chequer Bridge and past Chequer House Farm, all the way to the signpost at the T-junction.

2 Turn left on the tarmac bridleway; bear slight left at the old airstrip and slight left downhill. Continue through Scotton to the Chesterfield Canal at Osberton Lock.

3 Turn right then left under Bridge 49, and follow the overgrown towpath with the canal to the right.

4 Continue beneath the modern bridge carrying the A1, along the towpath opposite Ranby to the road left of Bridge 51. Turn left back up the road to the starting point and your vehicle.

42:A

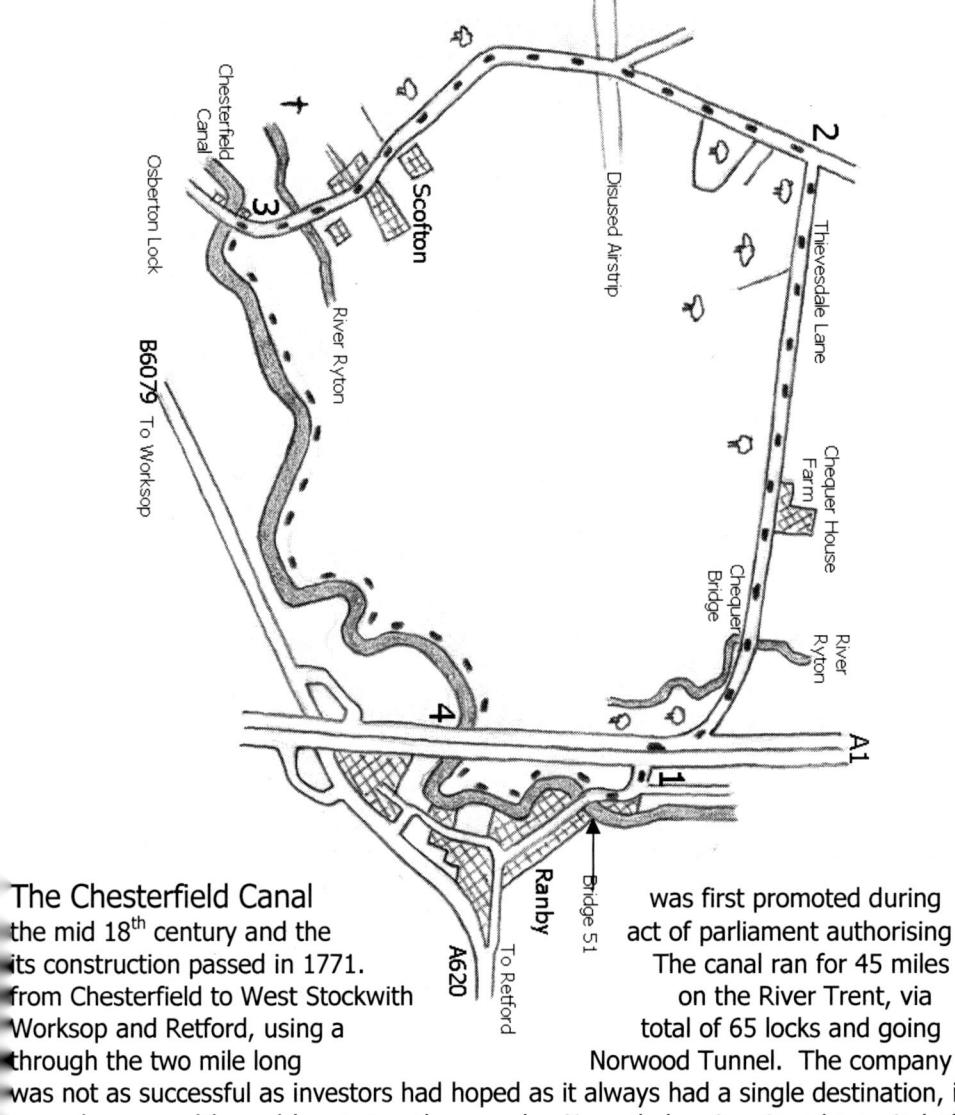

The Chesterfield Canal was first promoted during the mid 18th century and the act of parliament authorising its construction passed in 1771. The canal ran for 45 miles from Chesterfield to West Stockwith on the River Trent, via Worksop and Retford, using a total of 65 locks and going through the two mile long Norwood Tunnel. The company was not as successful as investors had hoped as it always had a single destination, it never became a 'through' route to other canals. Nevertheless it enjoyed a period of relative prosperity until the advent of the railways.

The roof of Norwood Tunnel collapsed in 1907 and has never been reopened; the canal, now shortened in length to 31miles struggled on through the first half of the 20th century. Paradoxically, as business use trailed off in the early 1950s, the canal gradually became popular with pleasure craft. It is now used extensively, particularly at weekends; it has had several locks rebuilt and other sections totally restored.

8 Swinston Hill Wood

$7^1/_4$ Miles $3^1/_2$ Hours

Park in either of the lay-bys on the A57 at Lindrick Dale, three miles west of Worksop. No facilities.

1 Start along the grass verge of the eastbound (north) side of the road heading towards Worksop. Just past the bus stop turn left at the footpath signpost and follow the path through the trees, bearing left at the marker post. Turn left along the wider stony track and turn right at the junction by the first telegraph pole. Keep direction on this track through Dewidales Wood and all the way to the road.

2 Turn left for 85yds to the footpath signpost and turn right straight across the field which may be under cultivation although a path should be well marked within any crop. Go into Swinston Hill Wood and take the track at the junction second right up a short slope, keep direction over the staggered junction and carry on ahead to the road at the top corner of the wood.

3 Cross and continue over the field ahead (a track should be visible) to the far side and turn right along the bridleway Brands Lane with the hedge to the left. Keep left of the marker post and the small stand of trees and continue to the road.

4 Turn left for six hundred yards, past the Gildingwells signpost to the bridleway signpost on the right. Turn right along the farm road past the double metal gate and follow this track right then left, continue for two thirds of a mile to the yellow topped post close to the trees.

5 Turn right through the hedge gap and go down the wide field edge with the trees to the left, to the four way signpost at the five way junction. Turn right along the track between fields and go straight on across the field ahead (a track should be well marked). Follow the hedged track all the way to the road at Woodsetts.

6 Turn left and immediate right at the signpost up the field edge with the houses to the right. Pass the marker post and keep ahead between the fence and the hedge, carry on along the tarmac drive to the bridleway signpost at a T-junction.

7 Take the road to the right, keep direction past a signpost at a junction and bear right/straight on, with the houses still right. Continue ahead on the narrower track and fork right, go through a gate and cross over the stony road. Carry on, bearing left on the path used earlier to the A57, turn right along the grass verge to the lay-by and your vehicle.

Page Nineteen

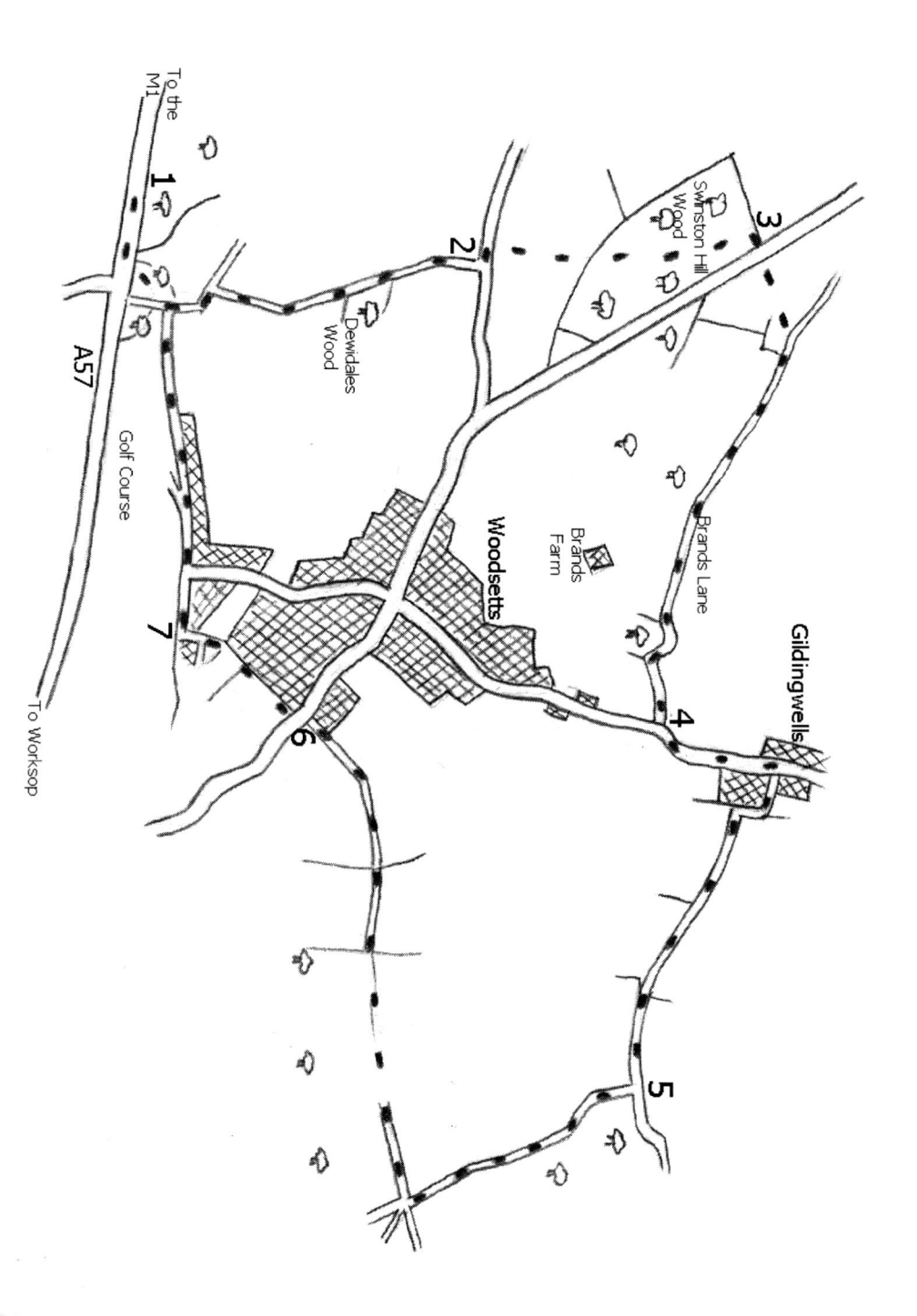

9 Hanger Hill Drive

7^1/$_2$ Miles   3 Hours

Park in Edwinstowe, at Swinecote Road (B6034) next to the funfair and the Art and Craft Centre (café inside). Toilets and other facilities in the town (quarter of a mile).

1 Take the bridleway signposted to Gleadthorpe. Continue through the trees with the field to the left, turn left/straight on at the junction for the Major Oak and keep direction at the angled junction over the Robin Hood Way. Bear left past the horseshoe marker post and the signpost.

2 Go past the metal barrier, turn right along the wider more substantial track and continue for two thirds of a mile to the crossroads. Turn left (signposted Warsop) past the metal barrier for a third of a mile to the signpost at the crossroads.

3 Turn left along the tarmac surfaced Hanger Hill Drive for nearly a mile to a marker post on the right, turn right and bear immediate left on a wider hardcore forest road. After three quarters of a mile at the three way signpost, go straight on along the lesser path past the Robin Hood Way marker disc.

4 At a junction a quarter of a mile further on, marked only by a yellow concrete 'H' post, turn left. Continue on this path along the edge of the trees with the fields to the right all the way to the A6075.

5 Cross this surprisingly busy road and take the tarmac bridleway ahead, (signposted Clipstone). Walk past the ornate gate house and follow the hardcore track to the signpost by the bridge.

6 Turn left on the path with the River Maun to the right and maintain direction on the path between the hedge and the trees away from the river. Carry on along the left hand field edge, hedge still left up to the bridleway signpost 20yds right of this track. Keep ahead along the right hand edge of the playing field.

7 Go through the gap and bear left and right between the houses, walk up to the end of Sixth Avenue. Turn left, then right at the junction along Fourth Avenue; turn right at the end and immediate left, up the High Street and cross at the traffic lights. Continue along Church Street, turn left back to the car park and your vehicle.

The silver-washed fritillary, with a wingspan of up to 70mm is the largest of the fritillary butterflies. It had been in decline for much of the last half of the 20th century but is now re-establishing itself in woodland areas throughout England. The butterfly is named for the silver streaks along the underside instead of the silver spots of most fritillaries.

Hanger Hill Drive

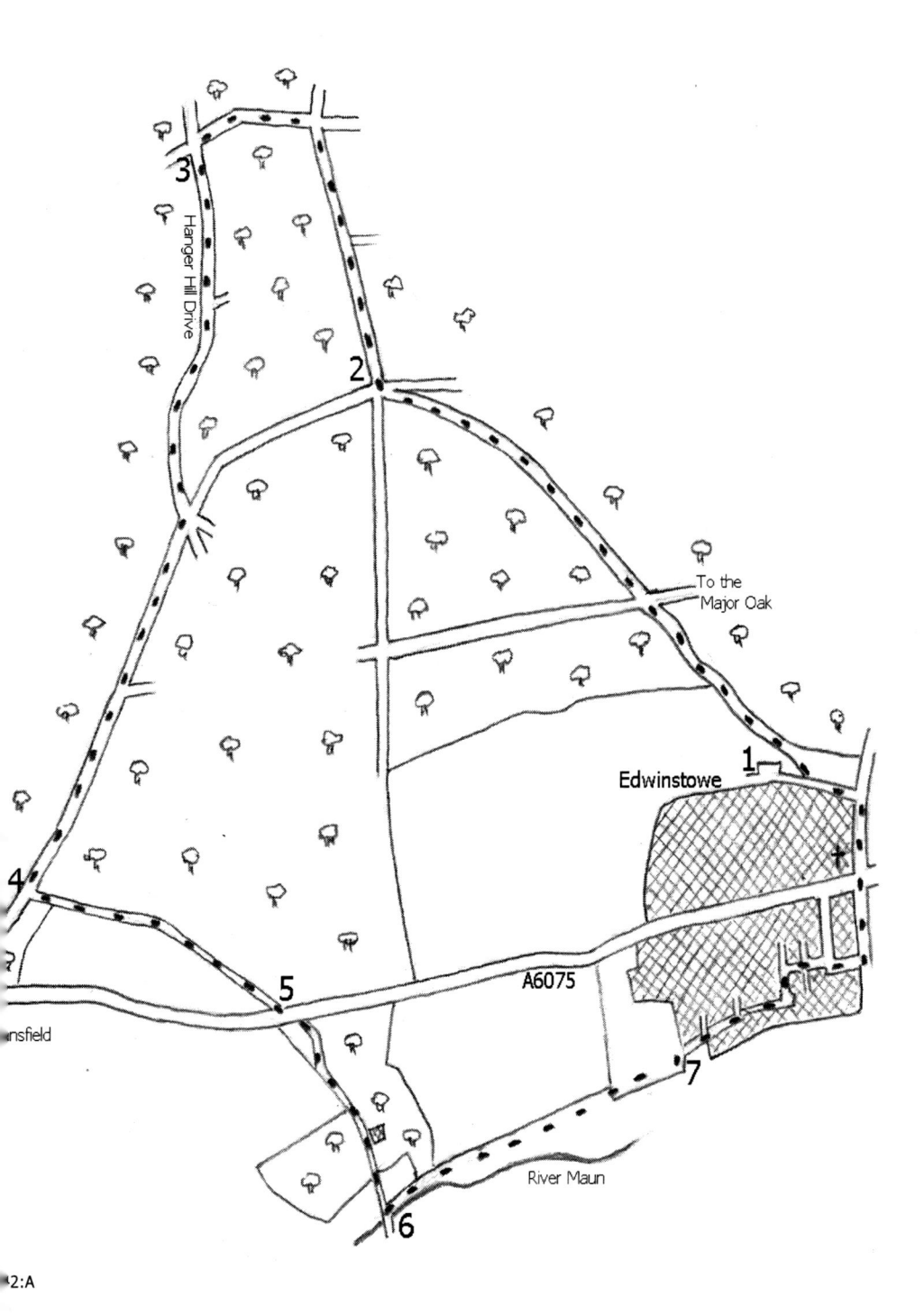

To the Major Oak

Edwinstowe

A6075

Mansfield

River Maun

Page Twenty One

10 Pleasley Vale

5^1/$_4$ Miles   2^1/$_2$ Hours

Use the Archeological Way car park, on the minor road to Pleasley Vale signposted off the B6407 east of Pleasley. Free but no facilities.

1 Take the footpath out of the car park through the trees, parallel to the road towards Pleasley Vale, with the road to the left. Go through the kissing gate at the crossroads of paths, carry on ahead over the stile on to the road and turn right.
2 As the road turns right, into the Vale, turn left past the heavy metal gates. Continue past the buildings and the next metal gate through the trees with the wood, Pleasley Park to the right. Keep direction to the road, cross and carry on ahead along the bridleway, Forge Lane.
3 Turn sharp right just before the road down the hedged bridleway, Green Lane and continue over Common Lane to the next road. Turn left/straight on, past the houses, through the metal gate and ahead along Wood Lane. At the roundabout keep direction on the path/cycleway and the road beyond, bear right at the junction up to the new road and cross over.
4 Go past the high, heavy iron gates and continue along the hedged driveway. Follow the road to the right around Littlewood and keep straight on over the fence when the road swings left again. Continue with the hedge to the left, step over the stile in the wall and carry on along the track with the cliffs to the right through the kissing gate to the access drive.
5 Cross and bear slight right between the narrower stream and the trees, go through the field and exit through the kissing gate at the far end. Keep on the tarmac road ahead as it winds through Pleasley Vale past the dark satanic mills to the gatehouse. Turn left along the path between the river and the trees back to the car park and your vehicle

Pleasley Park was a royal deer park in medieval times; it is now looked after by Forest Enterprise. The mill buildings in Pleasley Vale were built in the 18th century for the manufacture of cotton and silk fabrics. The complex has now been converted for office and industrial use.

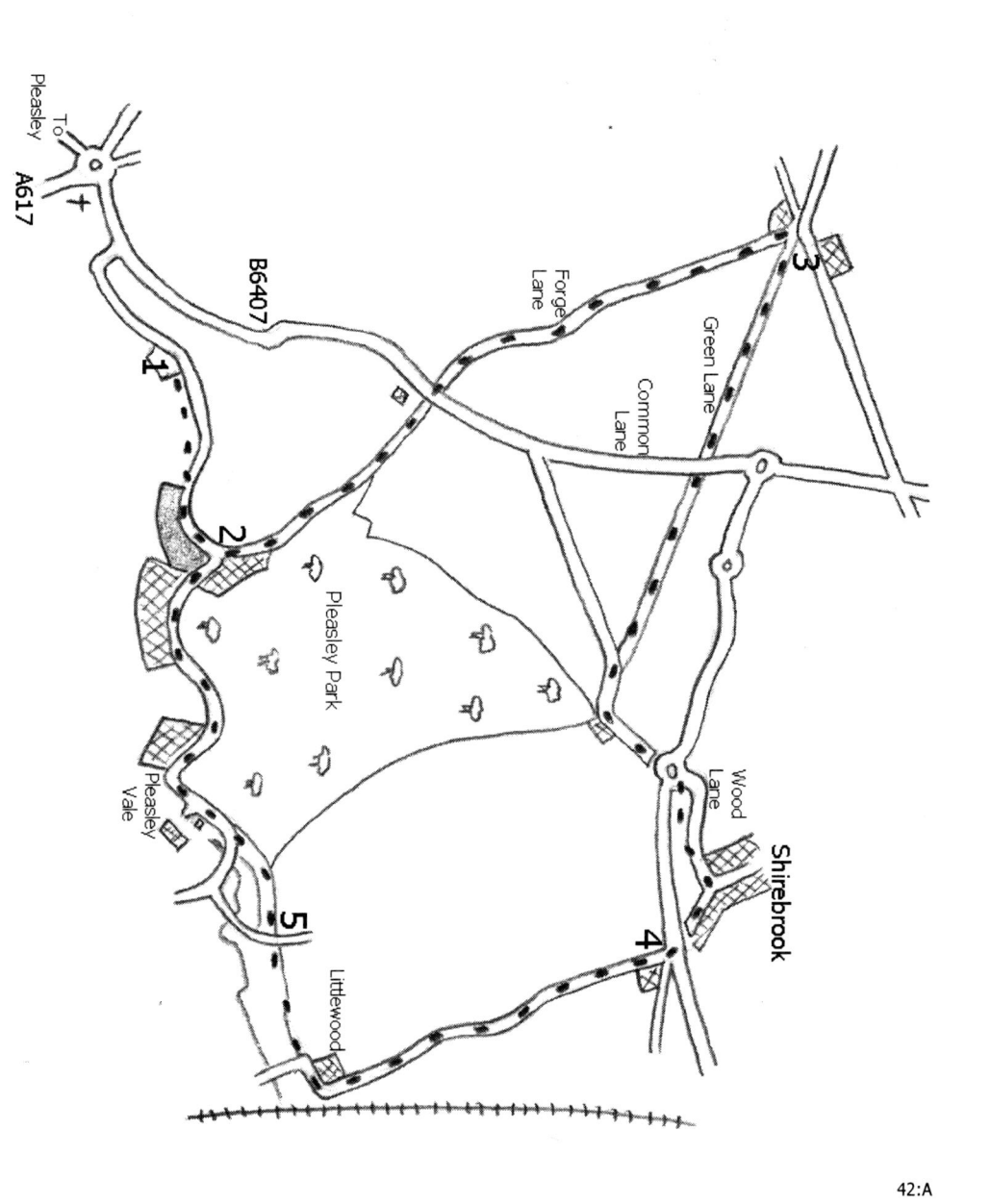

Pleasley Pit started producing coal in 1875, after its closure in 1983 a steam winding engine was preserved; it is now being restored by a group of enthusiasts.

Page Twenty Three

11 Rhodesia

5½ Miles   2½ Hours

Park in the country park area off Shireoaks Road, Shireoaks, no facilities.

1 Walk back towards the village, across the bridge over the canal and turn left down the road to the sports centre. Keep ahead in the corner, through the hedge gap and over the stone bridge. Bear right, along the edge of the field further away from the stream, with the hedge to the right and continue to the road.

2 Cross and go up the rough tarmac road ahead, as this road swings right into the derelict Hall, carry on past the metal gate step over the stile and bear left through the long grass to the top left corner. Go through the hedge gap and keep direction over the open field, which may be under cultivation although a path should be well marked within any crop, to the left hand end of the trees of Scratta Wood.

3 Continue through the end of the wood, along the edge of the trees and the left hand field edge. Carry on to the road with the trees of the second half of Scratta Wood to the right and turn left for 400yds to the footpath signpost.

4 Turn left, down the right hand field edge with the trees to the right, go through the boundary and turn right through the hedge gap at the marker post. Take the right hand field edge all the way to the road and turn left to the factory entrance.

5 Turn right and bear immediate right past the concrete bollard along the hedge lined tarmac track with the quarry to the right. Keep ahead past two marker posts and bear left off the road at the third, turn right past the next marker post through the trees with the wire fence to the right. Continue direction over the stony road with the wire fence now left, up to the railway. Cross and follow the overgrown hedged path ahead to the right of the house.

6 Step over the stile left of the metal gate and go down the farm track on the right hand field edge. Carry on over the boundary to the bottom right corner, go through the hedge gap and turn right along the hardcore road, through the metal gate up to the rough tarmac road at Manor Lodge.

7 Turn sharp left, go past another metal gate along the road past Lady Lea Farm and continue up the narrow hedged path into Rhodesia village. Turn left on Tylden Road under the railway bridge to the stile in the corner. Cross the field to the opposite corner, go through the gate and keep direction along the field edge over a stile; carry on into the corner with the trees to the right.

8 Bear left along the bottom of the canal embankment and cross to the left hand far corner. Step over the stile, follow the path through the undergrowth and continue past the house and the sports centre. Carry on ahead and then right back to Shireoaks Road; turn right over the canal back to the park and your vehicle.

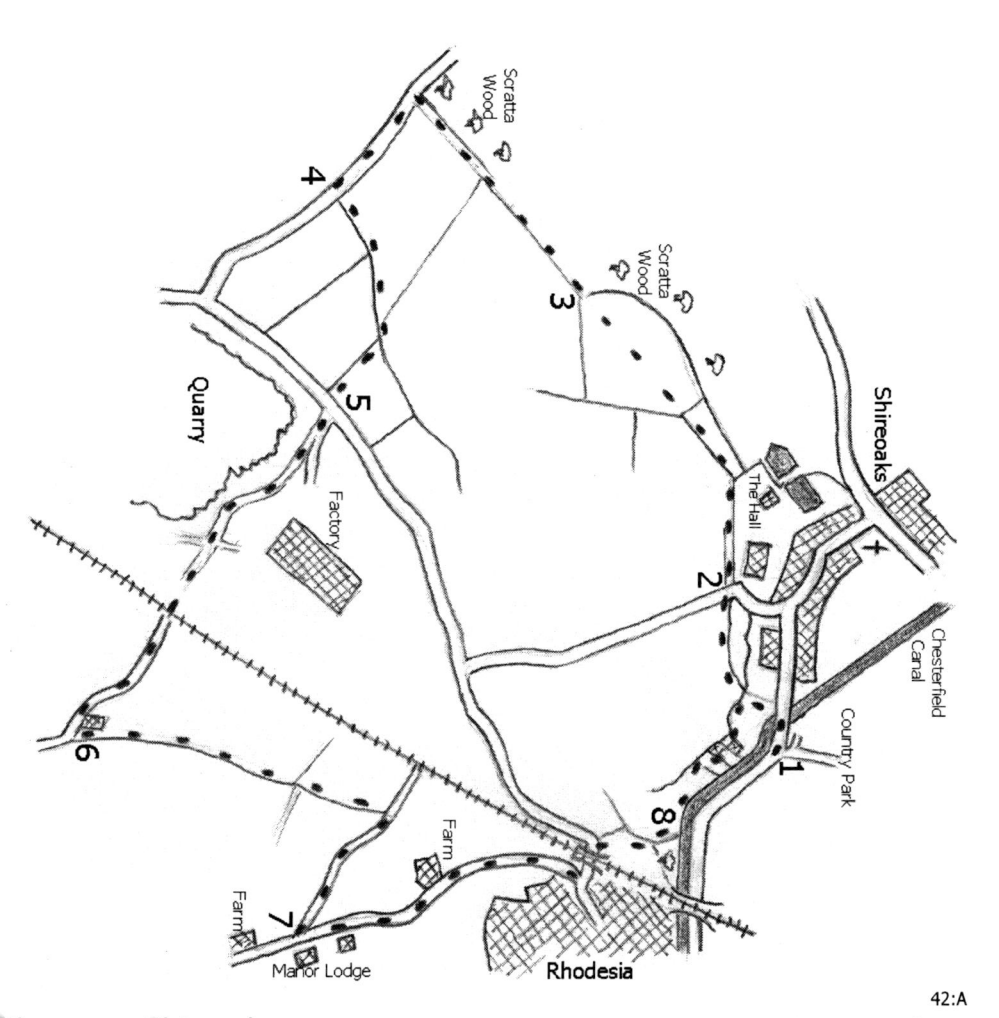

The name Shireoaks comes from an old oak tree which stood at the point where Yorkshire, Nottinghamshire and Derbyshire meet.

The Duke of Newcastle organised the first extractions at what was to become Shireoaks Colliery in 1854. The site had been chosen for its good rail and water links for transportation after a test shaft had been sunk nearby a few years earlier. It was producing coal from 1859 all the way through to closure in 1991.

Rhodesia village was built in the 1920's to house workers at the local mines at Shireoaks and Steetly. It was named after the chairman of the colliery Mr G Rhodes; the main village street, Tylden Road was named after the colliery manager Charles Tylden-Wright.

12   The Meden and the Maun

7 Miles   3 Hours

Park in the small car park/lay-by on a corner south of Bothamsall on the B6387 road to Ollerton. No facilities.

1   Leave the car park out of the back along the track past the green barrier. Bear right under the railway bridge on the field edge with the River Maun to the left. Carry on to the signpost, turn right then left along the farm road up to the junction. Turn right and follow the farm road down through the trees and bear left to the marker post.

2   Turn right through the narrow hedge gap and up the path with Bevercotes Beck to the left. Turn right in the corner and continue direction on the left and then right hand field edge. (The path officially goes diagonally across the field). Go through the wide gap in the corner and turn left along the left hand field edge through the corner to the marker post by the pylon.

3   Turn right and walk up to the road, turn right and follow the field edge parallel to the road for 125yds. Turn left over the road and go straight on along the bridleway between hedges; cross the railway bridge and continue ahead keeping the hedge and the trees to the right up to the signpost at the top corner.

4   Turn right and bear immediate left between trees with the wire fence to the left. At the crossroads turn right (there is an open field to the right after 150yds) and keep straight on; go downhill and bear right past the first footbridge, carry on with the River to the left and turn left over the second footbridge.

5   Continue ahead between the river and the trees and bear right with the track at the marker discs with the trees still on the right. After three quarters of a mile follow the farm track left, across the brick bridge over the River Meden and up to the road in Bothamsall.

6   Turn right along the road up to the church and bear left along Church Lane and continue direction on this road then track to Haughton Park House Farm. Turn right down the gentle slope to the road and cross over.

7   Walk down the drive across the bridge over the River Meden, under the railway bridge, past Haughton Hall Farm and over the River Maun to the signpost. Turn right and follow the track with the river to the right, back under the railway to the parking area and your vehicle.

Page Twenty Seven

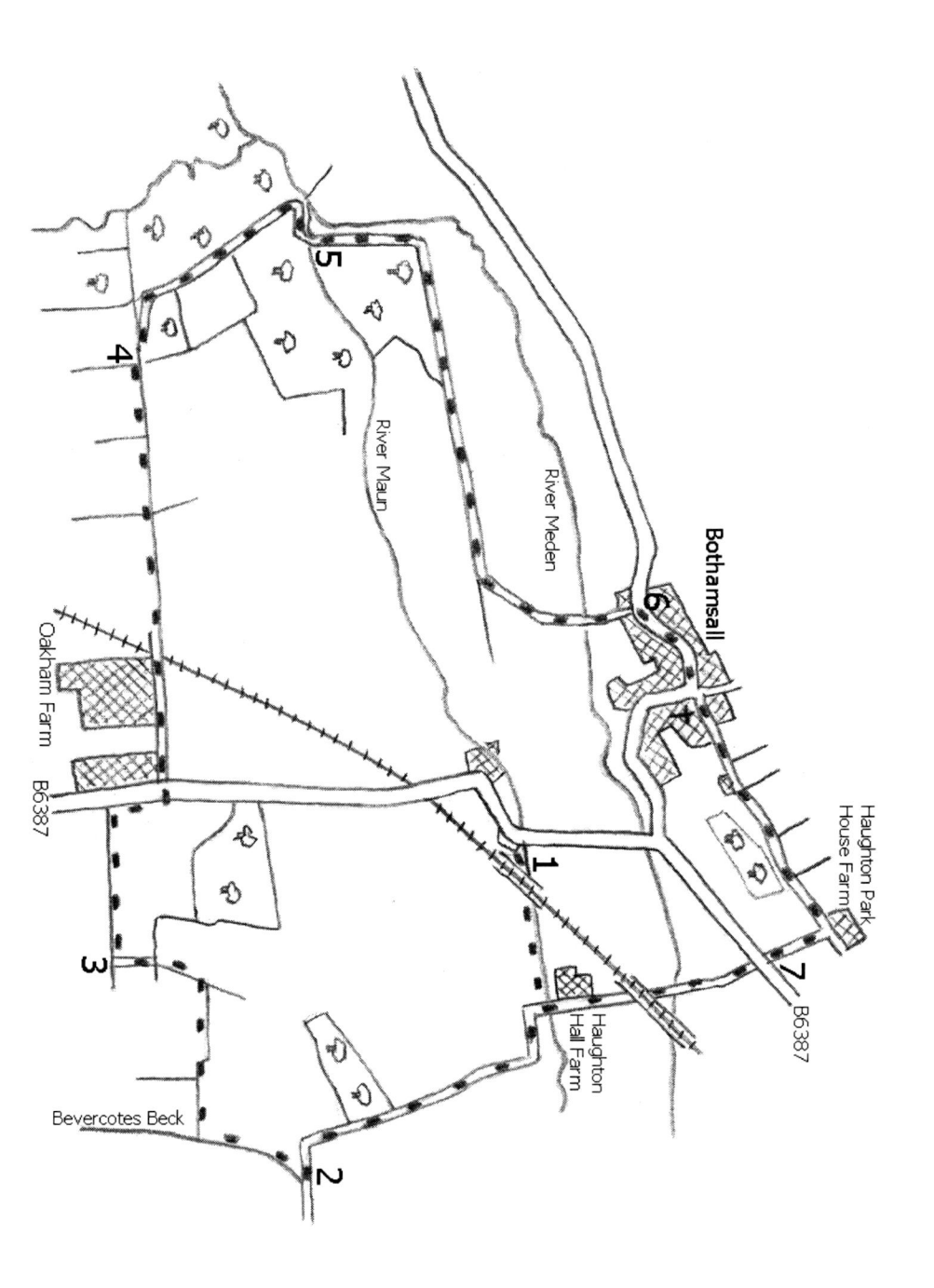

The 'Walking Close to' Series

Peterborough
The Nene near Peterborough
The Nene Valley Railway near Wansford
The Nene near Oundle
The Torpel Way (Peterborough to Stamford)
The Great North Road near Stilton

Cambridge
Grafham Water (Huntingdonshire)
The Great Ouse in Huntingdonshire
The Cam and the Granta near Cambridge
Newmarket
The Isle of Ely

Northamptonshire/Warwickshire
The Nene near Thrapston
The Nene near Wellingborough
The River Ise near Kettering
The Nene near Northampton
Pitsford Water
Rockingham Forest
Daventry and North West Northamptonshire
Rugby
Stratford-upon-Avon (Late Spring 2013)

Leicestershire
Rutland Water
Eye Brook near Uppingham
The Soar near Leicester
Lutterworth
The Vale of Belvoir (North Leicestershire)
Melton Mowbray
The Welland near Market Harborough

Bedfordshire/Milton Keynes
The Great Ouse near Bedford
The Great Ouse north of Milton Keynes
Woburn Abbey

Suffolk
Lavenham in Suffolk
Bury St Edmunds
The Stour near Sudbury
The Orwell near Ipswich
Dedham Vale
Stowmarket
Clare, Cavendish and Haverhill
Southwold and the Suffolk Coast
Aldeburgh, Snape and Thorpeness

Hampshire
Romsey and the Test Valley

Essex/Hertfordshire
Hertford and the Lee Valley
The Colne near Colchester
Epping Forest (North London)
Chelmsford

Wiltshire/Bath
The Avon near Bath
Bradford-on-Avon
Corsham and Box
The Avon near Chippenham

Lincolnshire
The Welland near Stamford
Bourne and the Deepings
South Lincolnshire
The Lincolnshire Wolds (South)
The Lincolnshire Wolds (North)

Somerset & Devon
Cheddar Gorge
Glastonbury and the City of Wells
The Quantock Hills
The East Devon Coast (Sidmouth, Branscombe and Beer)
Exmouth and East Devon

Norfolk
The Norfolk Broads (Northern Area)
The Norfolk Broads (Southern Area)
The Great Ouse near King's Lynn
North West Norfolk (Hunstanton and Wells)
Thetford Forest
North Norfolk (Cromer and Sheringham)

Nottinghamshire
Sherwood Forest
The Dukeries (Sherwood Forest)
The Trent near Nottingham

Oxfordshire/Berkshire
The Thames near Oxford
The Cotswolds near Witney
The Vale of White Horse
Woodstock and Blenheim Palace
Henley-on-Thames
Banbury
The River Pang (Reading/Newbury)
The Kennet near Newbury

Cumbria
Cartmel and Southern Lakeland

Hereford and Worcester
The Severn near Worcester
South West Herefordshire (Hay-on-Wye and Kington)
The Malvern Hills